T0129392

THE SKIN I AM IN

THE SKIN I AM IN

Alfreada Brown-Kelly

iUniverse, Inc.
New York   Bloomington

The Skin I Am In

This is a work of fiction. All of the characters, names, incidents, organizations, and dialogue
in this novel are either the products of the author's imagination or are used fictitiously.

iUniverse books may be ordered through booksellers or by contacting:

iUniverse
1663 Liberty Drive
Bloomington, IN 47403
www.iuniverse.com
1-800-Authors (1-800-288-4677)

ISBN: 978-1-4401-4133-1 (pbk)
ISBN: 978-1-4401-4134-8 (ebk)

Printed in the United States of America

iUniverse rev. date: 3/5/2010

CONTENTS

IN MEMORY

I dedicate this book to all of the people who have left me on earth to touch somebody's soul in a positive manner.

JUNIUS READO

VICTORIA BUTLER READO

OLIVER BROWN, SR

NORMAN EVERY, SR

CLARENCE BROWN, SR

MARY ELIZABETH ADAMS KELLY

MARGIE HILL

ACKWOWLEDGEMENTS

First of all I give thanks to my Lord and Savior Jesus Christ who does all things well and in a timely manner. My Lord, who cannot lie, and is the keeper of my soul; My Lord who is an on time God: My Lord who consistently and continuously blesses me even when I am not worthy of His numerous blessings…

To my beautiful daughter, Victoria Elizabeth Kelly… never give up on your dreams. I hope to see your book in print very soon…

To my husband, Ernest Kelly-keep motivating me…

Nieces and nephews…Kenneth Brown Jr., Brittany Brown, Schwanda and Kevin George, Crystal & Malik Jones, Justin Winston , Pierre Brown, Shairda Brown, Nicole Edwards, Jamie & Merrick Ferdinand, Chantelle & Terrell Collins, Mario, Denise and Gregory Dowl, Tiffany Woodson, Jordan Kelly, Brandon, Bryan and Brianna reach for the moon and the stars…anything is possible …

To BookClubEtc. and the ladies of W.I.N.E. (Women in Natural Essence) book club…I thank you for your continued support of me…

To all of the women and men who share their stories with me because some of the things I have written relates to them in some way…

Juanita & Lawrence Hill who are my extended family in the Big Easy…

Janice Washington and Cassandra Coney…true sisters who have my back…

Mr. Louis Johnson, my Editor… thanks for everything and <u>all</u> you do everyday…

To my Gethsemane Baptist Church family…I thank and praise God for your continued support.

To everyone who thought enough of me to buy my book for whatever reason. I love all of you…

Peace & Blessings, Alfreada Brown-Kelly

Time cannot be replaced.

Use
        Yours

                        Wisely……

CONTENTMENT

You make me purr like a kitten
I stretch lazily
When you stroke my ego
And stimulate my intellect
I savor the moments
When you enter in my space
And capture my undivided attention
With mesmerizing words
And subtle innuendos
You make me
Purr like a kitten

I SURVIVED

I survived
Through thick and thin
And all the chaos
In between
It was by His grace
The idea…………..
I could see His face
In the special place
You know
On the throne
In His heavenly home
In that place called heaven
Streets filled with gold
Angels walking tall
Talking to God
I survived
The unexplained
All the crazy games
I survived

YOUR ANGEL

Sometimes in your life
God will send someone
To give you a word
So His will can be done

That someone
Will be strong
Encourage everyone to get along
Differentiate between right and wrong
Sing a praise song

That someone
Will have a heart of gold
A spirit that is bold
A compassionate soul
A superhero role

That someone
Will love all races
Judge fairly in all cases
Knowledgeable and spiritual
On a continuous basis

That someone
Will be your angel.

IF

If you hurt me
I may break
They hurt Him
He recuperated

If you lie to me
I will cringe
They lied on Him
He rose again

If you steal from me
I will be mad
They stole from Him
He still was glad

If you don't acknowledge Him
You will fail
If you acknowledge Him
You will prevail

If you don't believe
In His holy word
You will never intimately know
The MASTER OUR LORD

THE MASTER

When all else fails
Call on the Master's name
He hears our every prayer
Each time we speak His magnificent name

When we look to our friends on earth
For answers to our woes
That is when problems begin
Not to mention the chaos

There is no one like our Master
On the earth below
Or the heavens above
Something we all know
Is His everlasting love

Try the Master for yourself
You will not be disappointed
He is the Alpha and the Omega
The one who is anointed

STILL WAITING

I am waiting
For you to become the man
That God destined you to be
A mighty warrior
Constant provider
Nurturing father
Loving husband
Anointed servant of God

I am waiting
For you to take control
Of every aspect of your life
Your inner most self
Your ability to advance
Your willingness to serve
In the kingdom of God

I am waiting
For you to see the light
From God's perspective
Fully understand
That without Him
You cannot and will not survive
I am still waiting

I GOT OUT

Trapped
In a small space
Inside my mind
Battered by angry words
Deceit and dishonesty
No love and even less hope
I got out

THAT MAN

Most women desire a man
To make them feel safe and warm
Calm their fears and relax their minds
Massage their bodies so they can unwind
A touch and a kiss that is so divine
Top it off with a glass of wine

A knight in shining armor
That will protect them from all hurt and harm
Stand beside them in the midst of their storms
His very presence gives them a sense of calm
Hearing his voice erases their fears and tears
Makes her feel like she doesn't have a care

That man who will touch
The very core of their souls
My! My! My!
We want that man
The one who understands
That with his presence
And very essence
He makes us feel safe, secure and protected from all
harm

WATCH OUT FOR THAT MAN

Watch out for that man.

The one who understands
You need a friend
One who will stick by you
Through thick and thin
Watch out for that man

He belongs to her…………..

Watch out for that man

The one who wiped your tears
Chased your fears
Knew you needed a caring touch
Offered you his love and ooh so much
Watch out for that man

He belongs to her

Watch out for that man

He just sits and waits
For your man to mess up
And exhibit no faith
To the woman he promised
To love till deaths do they part
He decided to share
Part of his heart
With you
Watch out for that man

He belongs to her

Watch out for that man
When you fall down
He will make sure he is around
To pick you up
And promise so much
But- watch out for that man

He still has to go home to her…..his wife

WHY DO WE

Why do we
Keep blaming them
For our stupidity
Ignorance and hatred
We
Are keeping us
Down and out
We
Are our own worst enemies

They
Work together
Help each other
And make sure
They work together
And help each other
Make sure
They move onward and upward

But we
Talk about each other
Backstab each other
Gossip about each other
And refuse to encourage each other
And make sure
We don't help each other get more than we do

Then
We are quick to say
They keep us down
They promote their own
And you know what
They do and we don't

We
Are Our Own Worst Enemies

Wake up People

AFTER THE REALIZATION

On the day I realized
You couldn't possibly love me
Because you didn't love yourself
I released myself
As a butterfly
Emerging from its cocoon
Flying free in the universe
And
I never looked back.......................................

IN THE END

Sandwiched between hope and fear,
Regrets and disappointments,
Coupled with a lack of love
And no hope for tomorrow
I bowed my head and prayed.

WHERE ARE THE DAYS OF YESTERYEAR

Where are the days of yesteryear?
When we didn't have any cares
When you refused to make a move
If I were not by your side
The love we shared
We could not hide

Where are the days of yesteryear?
We played and dreamed
Without any fears
Our love so strong
Could not be broken
We knew without a doubt
It was more than a token
Of two people in love from the very start
The love we shared was deep in our hearts

Where are the days of yesteryear?

SIGNS OF THE TIMES

Looking at the news
You begin to comprehend
What the bible predicts
Will happen in the end
Tornados, earthquakes, rumors of war
Floods and disasters,
Plague, famine and more
The world is in a state of turmoil
If we do not pray all of us will fall

MY JOB

I love my job, I love my pay
I love the way the haters talk about me every day
I love my boss he is the best
Another name for him is Mr. Pest
I love my office and its location
As a result, I never go on vacation
I love my supervisor who writes me up
I smile and say thank you very much
I love Cruella, Fiona and Anastasia
Gloria and Lil Lotta who is late everyday
I love Ms. Becky who always says "well"
I think she is so very swell
I am happy to work here I am I am
I love my job like I love spam

I OFTEN WONDER WHY

I often wonder why
I let you make me cry
I have nothing to gain
But trauma and pain
You can't control your hands
So I devised a plan
I will go away and leave this situation
And prepare myself for better days
This is not called love
It is not of God
I know this is abuse
And you're the one who is confused
I have only one life
It will be stress free
I'm walking out the door
Love does not live here anymore.

Love is free.

If you are paying for love …

Something
          Is
                    Wrong!!

WHILE LYING IN YOUR ARMS

She used to feel safe
But now she is afraid
She doesn't know what she is doing
While lying in your arms

She used to feel sure
What they had was real
But now she is not sure
While lying in your arms

Things are changing
Before her eyes
She sees many things
She was blind to before
While lying in your arms

Now she has to decide
Before it gets too late
She's been strung along too long
While lying in your arms

GOODBYE

It has been indeed
Such a pleasure
To have entered
Into your presence
We have worked
Laughed and played
It is a shame
You cannot stay
We understand
That you must go
But there is one thing
You must know
Things will never
Be the same
Who will
Play my silly games
Call me often
Call me twice
I'll let you know
Who has been
Naughty and nice
So long my friend
I know you will do well
You have a friend

YOU HAVE SOWN BAD SEEDS

You have sown bad seeds

Lies
Deception
Betrayal
Dishonesty

You will reap what you have sown

Deceit
Corruption
Bitterness
Death

DEAR GOD,

Let me not concentrate on the people who have hurt me
Let me concentrate on your goodness and mercy

Let me not concentrate on what should have been
Let me concentrate on what I will do in your name

Let me not be dismayed and want to give up
Let me concentrate on your promises

Let me not fall by the wayside trying to get even
Let me meditate and concentrate on you and only you

God
Let your will be done and not mine
Let me allow you to do great work me
Purge all the things that are not pure and give me a clean
heart
Amen

KINGDOMFEST

Kingdomfest
An event designed
To restore your faith
Teaching and preaching
Restoration for all
You will be guaranteed
A Holy Ghost Ball

Divas and Saints
Teaching forgiveness and love
Bishops and leaders
Spreading the Word of God

Don't miss the opportunity
To praise god with the Gethsemane community
Give Him the glory, the honor and the praise
For the rest of our anointed, love fulfilled days

HOW MANY YEARS

How many years
Have I lived with a stranger
How many years
You put my life in danger
How many times
You said I love you
When in reality
It was not the truth
Why did you pretend
It was just you and me
When you knew all along
It was a lie
Now you tell me
I am to blame
For your many indiscretions
That's a shame
Forgive me for not believing
Anything you say
Nothing with us
Will ever be......

THE PRAYER

Father in heaven
I have been damaged
I still praise your name
My self esteem is low
I still praise your name
My family has betrayed me
I still praise your name
My faith is shaky
I still praise your name
My anger is at a boiling point
I still praise your name
My hope is hopeless
But-I still praise your name

Thank you for not giving up on me
Even though I do so quite frequently
God I thank you for being the awesome, true and living
God, prince of peace, mighty healer and deliverer,
that is always on time and never late and whose mercy
endures forever. I thank you, praise you, and glorify your
wonderful, marvelous and magnificent name.
Amen

THERE IS ONLY ONE OF ME

There is only one of me
Not enough to share
But enough for one
One who thinks one of me is enough
There is only one of me

**ALWAYS
BE
YOURSELF.**

**WHEN YOU BECOME
SOMEONE ELSE…..**

**THERE WILL BE A
PROBLEM…………………**

I HAVE BECOME AN EMPTY SHELL

When you stole my joy
I became an empty shell
I moved methodically through each day
Not trusting my instincts to guide me
I have become fearful and I no longer feel safe
Faith is nowhere to be seen and hope does not exist
I have become an empty shell……..

A MOTHER'S LOVE

A mother's love is irreplaceable
Can never be erased
Will never fade
Always remain true
No matter what you do
Her love for you can never be broken
Cannot be stolen
Never get old
Pure like 24 karat gold
A mother's love is
Always and forever

YOUNG BLACK BROTHERS

Young black brothers
Stop killing each other
Then blaming the man
Like you don't understand
Now you are wearing orange
Or stripes
Having no rights
Placed in a cage
Destined to fight
To keep dignity and pride
Embarrassment aside
Making family cry
Think before acting
And behaving like a criminal

SUNDAY MORNING

Sunday morning
In all its glory
Like a cool breeze
Caressing your soul
Stirring emotions
Reflections
Of abundant blessings
The calmness
And inner peace
Surrounding you
On a Sunday morning

MY MOTHER

As I watch this woman
Who is responsible for my existence
I smile to myself
I will be her one day
Her memory not as strong as it used to be
Is a gentle reminder to me
I forget sometimes and I am younger than she
We laugh and talk about
Family members and yesteryear
Holding close in our heart
Memories that are dear
I watch my mother sit in her favorite chair
And thank God for her because she is the reason I am
here

WITHIN THE RECESS OF MY MIND

You have always been lodged within the recess of my
mind
When I abandoned you and went with him
You did not leave me
You were always there lodged in the recess of my mind
You waited and watched
When he disappointed me
You reappeared
And then you retreated within the recess of my mind

One time I couldn't find my way
You peeped around the corner in the recess of my mind
You hoped that I would make the right decision-but I
didn't
So you retreated within the recess of my mind

Another time I thought I was in love
I saw you smiling in the recess of my mind
You hoped that I had finally found peace
But the idea of love didn't materialize
Again you reappeared from within the recess of my mind

THE VISION

The man of God had a dream
He knew He would need a special team
To pursue the vision of an extraordinary church
One geared towards healing and teaching, and above all, putting
God first
Down on our knees
The Saints of Gods prayed
The Lord our God
Would meet our needs in a special way
We prayed in advance
For the souls that would be saved
We prayed to God
For all the decisions that were made
We prayed and magnified
Our Lord's Holy name
For the things He is going to do
In Jesus magnificent name
We fasted and prayed
From sun up to sun down
We prayed some more
For the breaking of the grounds
The man of God
Urged us to let god take control
For this would be the beginning
Of saving many lost souls
By fasting and praying
And doing His will
The Saints of God
Will be the first to tell
When you're doing work for God
And give Him all the glory
In the end
You'll be victorious
In God's victorious story

Sometimes

                  Hope

Is all we have......

It's all we need.

Live life to the fullest…

And then

Live some more…..

THE FIXER

I have always been a person who fixed things. I want to fix broken things, broken people and broken pieces. It has been a long and bumpy process, but I have come to the conclusion that fixing things is not one of my best assets. I hate to admit it, but I have messed things up trying to fix them. I didn't discriminate.......I was my first project. I had a plan. But, do you know that God is the man with the master plan. God has the blueprints. His plan transcended mine on every level. I *had* to let God *be* God. That meant I had to remove myself and allow Him to do his job. There is nothing too big or too small for God to fix. God can fix all things. And when God fix things, they are supremely excellent.......perfect. He, the Master carpenter, can put broken things and broken people back together again. If you can't believe anything else, try Him for yourself.

DO THE MATH

Why do we as women think we need a man to validate us? We are smart, successful, beautiful and intelligent individuals. The devil has lied to us telling us that we need additional validation. Please do not misunderstand me. We, as humans seek companionship. But when you do find someone, make sure that someone will complement you and add to what you already have. Don't sell yourself short. A woman I once worked with told me that she preferred married men. I was horrified. I quickly informed her that she had a case of "no" self esteem. When I hear things like that I have to wonder if the person is on drugs. I asked her why would she want someone else's man, husband or significant other. She told me if he was happy at home he would not want to be with her. O ye of little understanding and obviously the child of a mother who didn't teach her the facts of life. A man is a man. If you are crazy and simple enough to open yourself up, a man will walk in and take everything you are crazy enough to give to him. And then he will go home to

Her. She will be the wife, fiancée or significant other. "Her" is the one whose name is on the deeds, insurance policies and bank accounts. You do the math. Him + Her = Them. YOU are nowhere in that equation.

THE BLAME GAME

Black people are my people. I love our music, our culture and our history. But I do not love when we constantly and consistently blame others for our failures in our lives. There was a time when we could not progress, we could not obtain an education, and we could not do. But today, we have no one to blame for our shortcomings and failures but us. We have access to many resources. And if you don't know how to get these resources, *ask somebody*. But stop blaming "THEM". Because "Them" come in all colors and nationalities. And when they come to the United States of America, the land of the free and the home of the brave, they make it. They build restaurants, alterations shops and purchase franchises. They open restaurants, braid hair open seafood markets and they encourage and push their kids to attend college or learn a trade. They do whatever is necessary to make the American dream a reality. They make it work for them. Just like they do it- you can do it too. Stop blaming "THEM"!

THE BATTLE IS NOT YOURS

Was there ever a time in your life you thought you were not going to make it? Did you question God and say, "Why me, God?" I am serving you God, paying my tithes and acknowledging you in every way. Then, when things don't go as we believe they should, we start blaming the devil. We have a tendency to blame everything on the devil. But, from personal experiences, I have learned that Sometimes God allow things to happen to us so that we grow, trust him more and seek his face. Sometimes he will bring us to our knees. Sometimes god will literally break you. And, in breaking you, he will make you a stronger and wiser individual. In the end you will come out looking and smelling like a rose. And we all know that a rose is a beautiful thing.

DO YOU KNOW THIS WOMAN

A strong woman-with superhero powers

A humble woman-praying at every hour

A loving woman-respecting her man

A gentle woman-her children respect, love and

understand

A tireless woman-making sure everything is okay

A grateful woman-thanking God for everything

A praying woman-giving thanks to the King

A faithful woman-discerning right from wrong

A Holy woman-singing a praise song

Do you know this woman?

READING THE BIBLE IN 90 DAYS

Reading the bible in 90 days

Was truly a blessing in many ways

The Old Testament people took my breath away

Complaining and whining, thinking Jesus wouldn't do what He said

Not following His law or doing His will

Roaming to and fro they couldn't keep still

The New Testament guiding us daily

Reminding us to trust in His words and not to forsake Him

As a result we are growing and getting stronger

Believing in His word, realizing He lives among us

Praying and fasting for the rest of our days

Remembering to acknowledge Him in all of our ways

A RELATIONSHIP WITH GOD

If you don't have a relationship with God

You will not have a relationship with man

If you don't have a relationship with God

Nothing will be clear, do you understand?

If you don't have a relationship with God

Things will spiral out of control

Without a relationship with God

You will never claim your soul

Have a relationship with God!

HIM

You are doing the things he used to do

Loving me

Holding me

Being supportive of me

And

Just being there for me

If you keep doing those things

I will forget ………. him.

LIMITATIONS

FOR US,

BY US

FOR   THOSE   WHO
ACHIEVE……..

THERE ARE NO
LIMITATIONS………

WE DON'T SET ANY

WHY CAN'T WE GET ALONG

What is it with all of us?

Why all of the crazy fuss?

Why can't we all just get along?

Become a tight knit group and super spirit strong

Hating ourselves and our very own

Our ancestors moan due to hateful seeds sown

Daily they see us hating each other

Troubling our souls with baggage and clutter

But look at them

United as one

Doing what they must

To get the job done

Working united together one and for all

Encouraging each other to stand up tall

Until we unite and work together

As one tight knit group-like birds of a feather

They will continue to succeed and watch us fall

And help us bang our heads against the wall

Clear this clutter

Cleanse it from your brain

It's only mental bondage

Of self hatred that remains.

UNTIL

Until we become united and do His will

Use our knowledge , talents and God given skills

Look to the hills from whence cometh our help

God's abundant grace and mercy and unlimited wealth

Without Him we will certainly fail

With Him we will certainly prevail

WATCHING YOU

Watching you standing there

In all of your glory

Reaching out to me

Knowing that

I need no persuasion

Just the open invitation

To walk into the space

That you have created

For the hours

We are about to share

And the anticipation

Of the delightful treats

Make me weak ……………………..

BLINDED

I was chained to the idea

That I couldn't make it without you

I wasn't worthy of love

Until I opened my eyes

And took a breath of fresh air

And opened my mind

To the endless possibilities

That I possessed

And

Realized

Every inch of my body

Was worthy of love

And if you could not love me

I would love myself

Because I am worthy

Of love.

IN THE END

I was created in His image

Born to do His will

Praise His name

The tears in my eyes

Imagining Him on the cross

Dying for all my sins

Knowing I don't always obey His words

Knowing if I want to see His face

And continue in His grace

I have to change my ways

And be like Him

Stay away from sin

Change my wicked ways

And obey His commands

Stop following man

Who has no shame

And playing silly games

That have no meaning

Because in the end

Only His way will stand,

And stand, and stand, and stand..........

THE UNKNOWN

Sometimes the quiet serenity

Quiets me

And I think

About the unknown

That is forever present

And close by

Reminding me

That something is about to happen…

TRUTH

The truth is so

Pure

Powerful

Honest

Desired

Wanted

Needed

Truth should be

Woven into your soul

Instilled in your heart

Meditated on

Told often

Pondered upon

And a constant in your life

And relationships.

LIES

Lies

Come in all

Colors,

Sizes,

Shapes,

Some are

Simple,

Complex

Some are

Smiling

Sad

Confused

Crazy

But

In the end

A lie

Is still a lie....................

CYCLE OF ABUSE

Why do you let him
Hit you in your face
He hit you so hard
You were a disgrace
Made you feel like
You were nothing without him
Kept you away
From your family and friends
Your self esteem
Went below zero
You forgot who were
Your real heroes
Friends tried to help
But you turned them down
Because the man who hit you
Didn't want them around
You became confused
He said he wouldn't hit again
But that was a lie
From the first word to the end
If you don't get out
And end the abuse
He will continue to hit you
Again and again

THANKSGIVING PRAYER

There is so much for me to be thankful for

My family, my friends, my Lord who loves me

The blood that was shed on Calvary

The angels that are constantly protecting me

His grace and mercy that guides forever

No weapons brought against me shall prevail

Even though they slay me -my spirit will not fail

The prayer partners who continue to lift me up

The preachers and Saints who bring the word

I am grateful and humbly thankful

DON'T SELF DESTRUCT

Why do we self destruct

Can we not believe and put our trust

In the hands of the willing and capable Master

Who is the ruler of all things

He is more than a brother

More than a best friend

The life He provides is for a reason

In return we should praise Him

Every season

It says in His word

He gives us everlasting life

So stop all the foolishness

Misery and strife

Taking your life in your hands

Is a big mistake

TO LIVE OR DIE

To live or die

Is the question

At the end of the day

When all has been said and done

And darkness settles in

You can choose

To live or die

I choose

To live

Or better yet

Not to die

2010-2011 Coming Soon................

WHY WOMEN WEEP

First of all, I thank my Lord and Savior Jesus Christ for all of the women who have taken time out of their daily schedules to assist me with this book. I had this idea in my head for a long time and then I started to dream about it. Then I started to talk about it. Then I started asking people-what do you think about the idea. The idea I had-was to ask 150 women about a time in their life they had to weep (happy or sad) and what impact this weeping episode had on their life. I called many of you and received various responds. Some of you told me that you could write a book about weeping , others wanted to know if I would use their names. It is imperative that everyone understand that this book is not about us. It is a tool for others to know that life happens. And the same things that have happened to us, have happened to others. As a result, we had to weep. But we are all strong survivors.......superior beings. Hopefully, after reading _WHY WOMEN WEEP_, we will all become stronger physically, emotionally and spiritually.

NOTES